12

Barcelona '92

**MAKING
A SPLASH**

In the steeplechase, compet...
must clear 2...
o...

TRACK EVENTS

Field events take place in the area inside the Olympic stadium's track.

There are two sorts of athletic events: field events, which involve throwing or jumping; and track events, which consist entirely of races. In the Olympic Games, there are 30 different track events, and each one is covered in this book...

In short-sprint races, athletes must stay inside their own lane, but in middle- and long-distance events, they can cross over into other lanes.

Olympic Stadium, Atlanta, USA, 1996

SUPER STATS

All of the track events at the 2008 Olympic Games will start and finish inside Beijing's National Stadium, which is commonly called the 'Bird's Nest'. The stadium can seat 91,000 spectators and could fit four jumbo jets inside it!!

ANCIENT ORIGINS

The first records of the ancient Olympic Games date from 776 BCE. At this time, just one competition was included. This was a track event known as the 'stadion', which consisted of a 192-metres running race. The first recorded winner (and the first recorded Olympic champion) was a cook named Koroibos.

The track consists of eight lanes. One full lap is 400 metres.

BRAVO PAAVO!

One of the greatest Olympic track athletes of all time was Paavo Nurmi (FIN) who won a total of 12 medals (nine gold and three silver) at the Games between 1920 and 1928. Nurmi competed in seven different middle- and long-distance events. Perhaps his most remarkable achievement was winning the 5,000-metres just 30 minutes after winning the 1,500-metres!

OLYMPICS FACT-FILE

Ƨ The Olympic Games were first held in Olympia, in ancient Greece, around 3,000 years ago. They took place every four years, until they were abolished in 393 CE.

Ƨ A Frenchman called Pierre de Coubertin (1863–1937) revived the Games, and the first modern Olympics were held in Athens in 1896.

Ƨ The modern Games have been held every four years since 1896, except in 1916, 1940 and 1944, due to war. Special 10th-anniversary Games took place in 1906.

Ƨ The symbol of the Olympic Games is five interlocking coloured ring. Together, they represent the five different continents from which athletes come to compete.

HOT STUFF

Wherever the Olympic Games go, the Olympic flame goes too! A burning torch will be carried all the way from Olympia in Greece, the site of the ancient Olympic Games. A relay team of 5,000 runners will transport the flame across the world to reach Beijing for the opening ceremony.

ympic flame,
oul, 1988

RUN FOR IT

One race with ancient origins is the marathon. This was inspired by the story of an ancient Greek messenger named Pheidippides, who ran 39 km to bring news of the great Battle of Marathon. Unfortunately, after delivering his message, Pheidippides died of exhaustion!

Marion Jones (USA)

DISGRACED STAR

Marion Jones (USA) was a hot favourite at the 2000 Sydney Games and told the press she could win five gold medals. At the Games she won three gold medals and two bronze medals, but was later disqualified. It was found she had been taking banned drugs to enhance her performance. She had to return all of the medals in October 2007.

DID YOU KNOW?

‽ Runners in the 100-metres hold their breath until the end of the race!

‽ In 1992, at the age of 32, Linford Christie (GBR) became the oldest person ever to win the 100-metres.

‽ The 1900 and 1904 Olympic Games included an even shorter sprint of just 60 metres.

Starting block

The starting blocks are fitted with pressure-sensitive pads. These can detect if an athlete starts moving before the starting pistol has fired. Each athlete is allowed to make one false start – but a second offence means instant disqualification!

STARTING ORDERS

At the start of a sprint race, the official in charge shouts 'On your marks'. When they hear this, the eight runners kneel down and place their feet in the starting blocks. The starter then shouts 'Set', at which the runners lift their hips, raise both their knees off the ground and wait for the starting pistol to fire.

THE 100-METRES

The shortest of the great sprint races, the 100-metres has been part of the modern Games ever since they began.

FANCY A DIP?

Have a good look at the 100-metres sprinters in action. If you watch closely, you will notice how they thrust their chests out just before they cross the finish line. This is known as 'dipping'. It pushes their bodies forward and knocks a couple of hundredths of a second off their time — which can mean the difference between winning gold and coming second!

SCANDAL!

Sadly, a few Olympic athletes don't play by the rules. One of the worst cases of cheating occurred in the men's 100-metres final at the 1988 Olympics. Ben Johnson (CAN) was first to cross the finish line in a new world record time. However, just three days later, he was stripped of both his medal and record when it was discovered that he had taken banned drugs to improve his performance.

ANIMAL OLYMPIANS

The fastest human athletes reach a top speed of around 40 km/h, but the cheetah can knocks spots off that. This powerful big cat can sprint at up to 100 km/h!

THE 200-METRES

The first half of this race is run on a bend in the track. It requires a special sprinting skill to maintain a steady running rhythm while turning to the left!

HAVING A GOOD TIME

The reigning men's Olympic champion in the 200-metres is Michael Johnson (USA). His winning time of 19.32 seconds at the 1996 Games in Atlanta not only won him the gold medal, but also set a new world record!

Michael Johnson (USA)

SUPER STATS

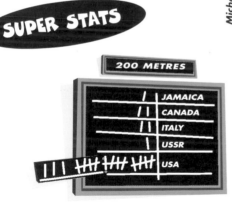

200 METRES

I	JAMAICA
II	CANADA
II	ITALY
I	USSR
III ₩₩ ₩₩ ₩₩	USA

The finals of the Men's 200-metres have been held 24 times at the Olympics. The Soviet Union (USSR) and Jamaica have both won once. Canada and Italy have each had two victories. The other 18 gold medals have all been won by the USA.

STAGGERING AROUND

Both the 200-metres and 400-metres have 'staggered' starts. This means that instead of lining up together in a straight line (as they do in the 100-metres), the runners in the inside lanes start behind those in the outside lanes. This compensates for the curve in the track and ensures that each athlete runs exactly the same distance.

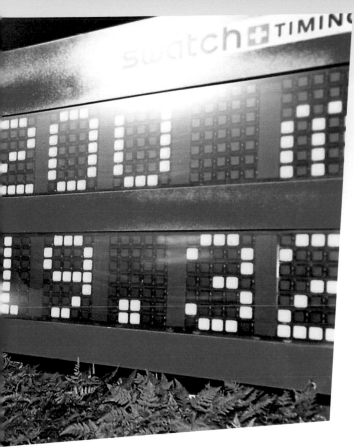

GOLDEN RECORD

Women competed in the 200-metres for the first time in 1948. The race was won by Fanny Blankers-Koen (NED) who also won the 100-metres, the 100-metres hurdles and the 4 x 100-metres relay. Her total of four gold medals at one games is a record for any female athlete!

Starting pistol

GOOD SHOT

The pistol used to start the 200-metres races is fired next to a microphone. The microphone carries the sound to speakers placed behind each of the starting blocks. This ensures that all the athletes hear the bang at exactly the same time. Without these speakers, the runner closest to the gun would hear it a fraction of a second before the others and get a head start.

DID YOU KNOW?

No man has ever won the 200-metres twice!

In 1904, the men's 200-metres was won by Archie Hahn (USA) after all the other runners had been given a 2-metre handicap for false starts!

In the 1932 final, one of the lanes used was 1.5 metres longer than all the others!

GOD SPEED

Eric Liddell (GBR) won the 400-metres in 1924 — despite the fact that he had spent months training for the 100-metres instead! Liddell was a devout Christian and refused to run in the 100-metres because the final was on a Sunday which the Bible says should be a day of rest. Remarkably, Liddell not only came first in the 400-metres, he also broke the world record.

Eric Liddell (GBR)

DID YOU KNOW?

♫ All races over 110-metres must be run anti-clockwise!

♫ In 1984, Valerie Brisco-Hooks (USA) became the first person in Olympic history to win both the 200-metres and the 400-metres at the same Games!

♫ A film called Chariots of Fire was based on Eric Liddell's story.

WORLD CHAMP

Marie José Pérec (FRA) won the women's 200-metres at the 1992 and 1996 Olympics but could not win for a third time in 2000. She lost to Australian runner Cathy Freeman, much to the delight of the host nation. However, Marie José Pérec still holds the Olympic record.

THE 400-METRES

This is the longest of the sprint races — and the toughest! Competitors run flat out all the way around the Olympic running track.

NO COMPETITION

In 1908, the men's 400-metres was won by Wyndham Halswelle (GBR). It was the easiest victory in Olympic history — because Halswelle was the only person in the race! He ran solo in a re-run after the original winner was disqualified and the other two finalists withdrew in protest.

LIGHT WORK

Originally, a thin piece of thread or tape was stretched across the finishing line. Nowadays, this has been replaced by an invisible beam of light. A sensor detects the moment that the light is broken by one of the runners crossing the line and automatically records the winning time.

Marie José Pérec (FRA)

ANIMAL OLYMPIANS

Modern Olympic athletes fly around the 400-metres running track in under 50 seconds. But a duck could fly around much faster! Ducks are among the fastest flying birds, with a top speed of over 100 km/h. This means they would take just 14 seconds to fly 400-metres!

THE 4 X 100-METRES RELAY

This race is all about teamwork. The teams are made up of four runners who each run 100 metres – that's a quarter of the race.

TAKE THE TUBE

Instead of messages, modern relay runners carry a short hollow tube called a baton. It's about 30 cm long and weighs at least 50 g – that's about as heavy as a golf ball. If a runner drops the baton during a race, they must pick it up again before continuing.

SUPER STATS

The women's world record in the 4 x 100-metres is just 0.59 seconds slower than four times the women's world record for the 100-metres!

Practising changeover

The moment when one runner passes the baton to another is called a 'changeover'. Relay runners spend many hours practising their changeovers to make them as smooth and fast as possible.

GET THE MESSAGE?

The origin of the relay races dates back to ancient times when important messages were sent over long distances using teams of runners. Each messenger would run as fast as he could until he reached the next member of the team. Then he would hand over the message to his team-mate who would run the next leg of the journey.

DID YOU KNOW?

The German team in the women's 4 x 100-metres relay missed out on a gold medal in 1936 because they dropped the baton!

Barbara Pearl Jones (USA) was a member of the winning US team in the 1952 women's 4 x 100-metres relay. At just 15 she was the youngest track athlete ever to win a gold medal!

Jesse Owens' amazing winning streak was repeated in the same events by another American, Carl Lewis, in 1984!

GOLDEN GREAT

Jesse Owens (USA) was a member of the US relay team that won the 4 x 100-metres in 1936. Owens also won gold medals in three individual events — the 100-metres, the 200-metres and the long jump!

Jesse Owens (USA)

SUPER STARS & STRIPES

The men's 4 x 400-metres relay was held for the first time at the Olympics in 1912. It was won by the USA, which has dominated the event ever since. In fact, the US team has won 16 out of the 21 finals. This picture shows them celebrating their most recent victory at Sydney in 2004.

USA men's 4 x 400-metres relay team

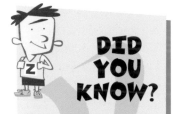

DID YOU KNOW?

♫ In 1988, Olga Brzygina (URS) won gold medals in the women's 4 x 400-metres relay and the 400-metres, while her husband Viktor won a gold medal in the men's 4 x 100-metres!

♫ The 4 x 400-metres relay is not run in lanes, so runners have to look behind them as they take the baton. Runners in the less chaotic 4 x 100-metres don't need to do this!

♫ The part of the race run by each member of a relay team is called a 'leg' – so you could say all relay runners have one leg!

BREAKING LANES

Unlike runners in the 4 x 100-metres relay, those in the 4 x 400-metres don't have to stay in their lanes. However, they must make sure that they don't get in each others' way – particularly in the changeover zone!

Relay changeover

THE 4 X 400-METRES RELAY

This relay is four times longer than the other Olympic relay race – which makes it four times as tough!

FIRST AND LAST

The first relay race ever held at the modern Olympics was a medley relay which took place in 1908. Instead of all the athletes running the same distance, the first and second runners ran 200 metres, the third ran 400 metres and the last ran 800 metres (a total of 1,600 metres). The race was won by the USA but was never held again.

ZONE LIMITS

Athletes must pass the baton to their team-mate inside the changeover zone. This stretch of track is 20 metres long and special markings show where it begins and ends. Competitors are allowed to start running before they have been handed the baton, but they mustn't pass beyond the end of the zone without it – if they do, their team will be disqualified!

SUPER STATS

Races have got faster and faster! The current men's world record is now more than 20 seconds faster than the winning time in the first ever Olympic 4 x 400-metres relay held in 1912.

THE 800-METRES

This is the first of the two middle-distance races held at the Olympics. It's a test of stamina as well as speed.

GIRL POWER

The men's 800-metres has been held at every single Olympic Games. The women's event was introduced in 1928 but wasn't held again until 1960. This was because the men who organized the Olympics were worried that women weren't strong enough to run such a long race. However, female athletes have since proved them wrong — in fact, the women's 800-metres record is now 18 seconds faster than the winning time in the men's event of 1896!

RUNNING FLAT OUT

The longer the race, the more exhausting it is for the runner. In the 1996 Games, Vebjorn Rodal (NOR) had used up all his strength by the end of the men's 800-metres final, as the picture shows. Still, it was worth it — he won the gold medal and set a new Olympic record!

Vebjorn Rodal (NOR)

ANIMAL OLYMPIANS

The common flea can cover 33 cm with a single jump. That's about 220 times the length of its own body. If humans could do the same, we would be able to complete the 800-metres with just two leaps!

MEN'S RECORDS - WORLD: Wilson Kipketer (DEN) - 1 min. 41.11 sec. **OLYMPIC:** Vebjorn Rodal (NOR) - 1 min. 42.58 sec.

Racing tactics

BOXING MATCH

Tactics play a big part in winning a race. A runner who doesn't watch out can end up being boxed in — in other words surrounded by a group of other runners and prevented from taking the lead. This is what has happened to the runner wearing number 151 in the picture.

DID YOU KNOW?

The 800-metres begins with a staggered start, but once the runners pass the first bend they are allowed to disregard their lanes and move to the inside of the track.

In 1992, the gold and silver medalists in the 800-metres men's final were separated by only 4/100th of a second!

The 1928 women's 800-metres was won by 24-year-old Lina Radke-Batschauer (GER) — the first individual gold medal won by a German competitor at the Olympics!

ON THE BALL

At the 1992 Games, the gold medal in the women's 800-metres was won by Ellen Van Langen (NED). However, Langen began her sporting career not as an athlete but as a football player! Four years before her Olympic triumph, she was playing in the Dutch national women's team.

Kelly Holmes (GBR)

All athletes must wear a number on their clothing. This is used by race officials to identify them.

A runner's clothing needs to be light and flexible. Tight-fitting clothes make the athlete's body more streamlined and aerodynamic.

THE 1,500-METRES

The men's 1,500-metres has been part of every Olympics since the modern Games began, but the women's event was not introduced until 1972.

DOING THE DOUBLE

So far, eight athletes have won both middle-distance races at the same Games. Kelly Holmes (GBR), pictured right, is the most recent. She took the gold in the 800-metres and the 1,500-metres at Athens in 2004.

MEN'S RECORDS - WORLD: Hicham El Guerrouj (MAR) – 3 min. 26 sec. **OLYMPIC:** Noah Ngeny (KEN) 3 min. 32.07 sec

Start of the 1,500-metres

GETTING GOING

Unlike shorter races, the 1,500-metres doesn't begin with a staggered start. Instead, runners form a curved line across the track and are allowed to break from their lanes as soon as the starting pistol is fired.

Runners wear lightweight shoes with short spikes on the sole. The spikes, which must not be more than 12 mm long, help to grip the running track and stop the athlete slipping.

SUPER STATS

The diplodocus was one of the longest dinosaurs that ever roamed the Earth, but it wasn't nearly as long as the 1,500-metres race! In fact, you would need more than 55 of these giant dinos placed nose-to-tail to reach from the start to the finish line.

SHORT-SPRINT HURDLES

*T*he short-sprint hurdles race requires total concentration. The smallest mistake can lead to disaster — as athlete Gail Devers discovered!

SPOT THE DIFFERENCE

In all hurdle races there are 10 hurdles to jump. The difference is in the height of the hurdle and the length of the track. The men's short-sprint event is 110-metres long — that's 10 metres longer than the women's event. The men's hurdles are also slightly higher — 106.7 cm compared to 83.8 cm.

GOING...

GOING...

GONE...

Gail Devers (USA)

FALLING AT THE FINAL HURDLE

In the 1992 Games, Gail Devers (USA) was in the lead during the final of the 100-metres hurdles when she hit the last hurdle with her foot. This mistake cost her the race. She lost her balance, stumbled and fell over the line in fifth place. Five days earlier, Devers had won the 100-metres sprint. Had she also won the hurdles, she would have become the first woman in Olympic history to take the gold in both events.

Liu Xiang, the reigning men's short-sprint Olympic champion celebrates after winning the gold medal at the 2004 Athens Games. It was his country's first gold medal in athletics since the Atlanta Games eight years before.

UP, UP & AWAY!

As a hurdler leaps over a jump, they push their front leg straight out ahead of them. Their other leg follows knee-first and is kept bent, sweeping low and flat over the top of the hurdle. Hurdlers must spend hours practising their jumping technique to ensure a perfectly smooth running rhythm.

Liu Xiang (CHN)

DID YOU KNOW?

In both the men's and the women's short-sprint hurdles, athletes take three strides between each jump.

Hurdlers are allowed to knock the hurdles down, but if their foot passes by the side of hurdle below the height of the crossbar they will be disqualified.

Until 1968, the women's short-sprint hurdles race was just 80 metres long.

WOMEN'S RECORDS - WORLD: Yordanka Donkova (BUL) – 12.21 sec. **OLYMPIC**: Joanna Hayes (USA) 12.37 sec.

THE ONE & ONLY

Only one athlete has ever won both the 400-metres and 400-metres hurdles. His name was Harry Hillman (USA) and he achieved this remarkable feat back in 1904. However, the hurdles used in Hillman's race were 15 cm shorter than the hurdles used today.

MIGHTY MOSES

Edwin Moses (USA) won the men's 400-metres hurdles at the 1976 Olympics and set a new world record. The following year saw the beginning of a winning streak for him which lasted almost 10 years! He won every single one of his next 122 races, including another Olympic gold in 1984.

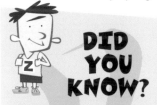

DID YOU KNOW?

⁇ The hurdles in the 400-metres are lower than the ones used in the short-sprint hurdles – 91.4 cm high in the men's event and 76.2 cm high in the women's.

⁇ Hurdles are designed so that they will fall over when the crossbar is hit by a force of at least 3.6 kg.

⁇ Edwin Moses would almost certainly have won another Olympic gold in 1980. However, US athletes refused to compete in the Games that year because of a political protest.

Edwin Moses (USA)

WARM-UP TECHNIQUES

All athletes have to warm up before they compete to help prevent injuries such as torn muscles. A good warm-up exercise for hurdlers is called 'ground hurdling'. This involves sitting down with one leg stretched out in front of you and the other bent around behind you, then bending forward as far as possible. Stretching a leg out along the top of a hurdle is also a good way to warm up!

The hurdles are shorter in this race, but sprinting for 400-metres is a big part of the challenge!

In the 400-metres event, the hurdles are placed 40-metres apart. The great Edwin Moses was capable of covering this distance in just 13 strides!

At 76 cm high, the hurdles used in the women's 400-metres are about half as tall as you are. But even the shortest hurdles are a tall order if you have to jump over 10 of them in a row!

SUPER STATS

Tony Jarrett (GBR)

THE STEEPLECHASE

At 3,000-metres long and with 28 hurdles and 7 water jumps to clear, the steeplechase is positively a hurdling marathon!

LEADING THE CHARGE

This picture shows Joseph Keter (KEN) lagging behind his countryman Moses Kiptanui in the 1996 Atlanta Games, but Keter then went on to win the race! Kenya has completely dominated this event — at the last six Olympics Kenyan athletes won six gold medals, five silver medals and two bronze medals!

ANIMAL OLYMPIANS

The steeplechase is named after a type of horse race which involves jumping over hedges and ditches. If horses were to race against humans, they would gallop away with the gold. They can run twice as fast and can clear jumps two-and-a-half times higher than the steeplechase hurdles.

Unlike the other hurdles, these ones are sturdy and can't topple over.

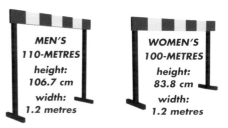

MEN'S 110-METRES
height: 106.7 cm
width: 1.2 metres

WOMEN'S 100-METRES
height: 83.8 cm
width: 1.2 metres

MAKING A SPLASH

Competitors jump straight over the hurdles but when they come to the water jump, they step on the crossbar. Leaping from the top of the barrier enables them to jump further and clear more of the water. However, it's impossible not to land with a splash, and everyone ends up with wet feet!

LANDING IN DEEP WATER

The bottom of the water trough is sloped so the water gets shallower the further you jump. The trough is deepest near the hurdle. The water here is 70 cm deep – if you stood in it, it would come up to your middle!

Joseph Keter (KEN)

DID YOU KNOW?

Only men take part in the steeplechase internationally. However, women compete in this sport at a national level in many countries.

To cover 3,000 metres takes 7.5 laps of the running track. Each lap has four hurdles and one water jump.

In the 1932 Olympics, the winner of the steeplechase ran an extra lap by mistake!

HURDLING HEIGHTS

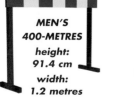

STEEPLECHASE
height: 91.4 cm
width: 3.96 metres

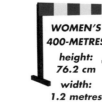

MEN'S 400-METRES
height: 91.4 cm
width: 1.2 metres

WOMEN'S 400-METRES
height: 76.2 cm
width: 1.2 metres

Steeplechase hurdles are the same height as the ones used in the men's 400-metres hurdles race. The hurdles are 3.96 metres wide – much wider than the hurdles used in other races. This is because all the competitors go over the same jumps.

LONG WAIT

Women athletes had to wait until 1984 before they could take part in long-distance races at the Olympics. A 3,000-metres race and women's marathon were finally introduced when the Games came to Los Angeles in 1984. Four years later, in Seoul, women were allowed to compete in the 10,000-metres for the first time. In 1996 the women's 3,000-metres was replaced by the 5,000-metres — which means, at long last, the women's and men's long-distance events are the same!

Junxia Wang (CHN)

DID YOU KNOW?

♫ Nowadays, athletes are given their medals in a grand ceremony in front of the crowd but when the modern Olympics first started, medals were sometimes sent out in the post!

♫ Athletes in middle- and long-distance races are not allowed to use starting blocks.

♫ There used to be a 5,000 metres team race. It was held only once, in 1900, when it was won by a team made up of British and Australian runners.

Atlanta 199

3154

MEN'S RECORDS - WORLD: Kenenisa Bekele (ETH) 12 mins. 37.35 sec. **OLYMPIC:** Saïd Aouita (MAR) 13 mins. 5.59 sec.

THE 5,000-METRES

When the going gets tough, the tough get going. And in a 5,000-metres race, they've got a long way to go!

WANG WINS

The first woman to win an Olympic gold medal in the 5,000 metres was Junxia Wang (CHN) at Atlanta in 1996. Her record has been broken twice since. Her winning time at Atlanta (1996) was just a fraction of a second under 15 minutes and set a new Olympic record.

IN TRAINING

Long-distance races test the athletes' fitness and stamina to the limits. Competitors have to spend countless hours training and run up to 150 km every week in order to stay in peak condition. That's the same as 375 laps of an Olympic running track!

FAMOUS FIVE

Five athletes have won both the 5,000-metres and the 10,000-metres at the same Games. Vladimir Kuts (URS) achieved this remarkable double when the Olympics were last held in Australia back in 1956.

Vladimir Kuts (URS)

ANIMAL OLYMPIANS

The pronghorn antelope is the long-distance running champion of the animal kingdom. It can maintain a steady speed of 56 km/h over a distance of 5,000 metres. No other animal can travel so far so fast!

THE 10,000-METRES

This is the longest race held inside the Olympic stadium – athletes have to cover 25 laps of the running track!

AFRICA UNITED

In 1992, athletes from South Africa were able to compete at the Olympic Games for the first time in 32 years! They had been banned until this time because of their government's apartheid policy which kept black and white people apart. However, when this policy was ended, so was the ban. Elana Meyer (RSA) celebrated her country's return to the Games with a silver medal in the women's 10,000-metres, finishing six seconds behind Derartu Tulu (ETH).

SUPER STATS

Travelling at top speed without taking any rests, it would take a garden snail more than eight days to finish the 10,000-metres!

Elana Meyer (RSA)

THINKING WITH YOUR FEET

Winning a long-distance race requires mental tactics as well as physical stamina. Runners have to plan how they are going to use their energy reserves. Some try to surprise their opponents with a sudden burst of speed a whole lap before the end of the race, while others save all their energy for the final sprint just before the finish.

DID YOU KNOW?

The current world record in the 10,000-metres is 5 minutes faster than the winning time in the 1912 Olympics!

Finland has won the men's 10,000-metres more times than any other country, with seven victories to its credit.

The 10,000-metres race takes more than 160 times longer to run than the 100-metres race!

SETTING THE PACE

World records in long-distance events are rarely broken at the Olympic Games. This is because all of the competitors are trying to win, so there's usually no one to act as a 'pacemaker' — someone who leads the race at the beginning and sets a fast pace for the others to follow. Pacemakers help other athletes break records, but because they start out so quickly they are usually exhausted before they reach the finish line.

WINNER'S SONG

At the 2004 Games Kenenisa Bekele (ETH) won the gold medal in 10,000 m and the silver in the 5,000 m. Bekele also holds the world record in the 10,000 m and even had a song written about him called *History is Made*.

Kenenisa Bekele (ETH)

WOMEN'S RECORDS - WORLD: Wang Junxia (CHN) – 29 mins. 31.78 sec. **OLYMPIC:** Derartu Tulu (ETH) – 30 mins. 17.49 sec.

FANCY A LONG WALK?

Walking races are very long! The women's event used to be 10 km, but ever since the Sydney Olympics it has been doubled to 20 km. There are two men's events. One is the 20-km and the other is the whopping 50-km (not competed by women) — that's longer than the marathon!

DID YOU KNOW?

🎽 The 50-km walk is the equivalent of 125 laps of the Olympic track.

🎽 There have been several other walking events in Olympic history — including a 1,500-metres walk!

🎽 Walking races start and finish in the Olympic stadium but most of the race takes place in the surrounding streets.

Women's 10-km walk

WIGGLE IT!

By swinging their hips from side to side, walkers can increase the length of their stride. This means they travel further with each step — but it also means they look quite silly!

Andrzej Chylinski (USA)

MEN'S RECORDS - WORLD: 20-km: Jefferson Pérez (ECU) – 1 hr. 17 mins. 21 sec. / 50-km: Nathan Deakes (AUS) – 3 hr. 35 mins. 47 sec.
OLYMPIC: 20-km: Robert Korzeniowski (POL) – 1 hr. 18 mins. 59 sec. / 50-km: Vyacheslav Ivanenko (URS) – 3 hr. 38 mins. 29 sec.

WALKING RACES

Walking races sound easy enough but there's a lot more to them than you probably think!

LEARNING TO WALK

In a walking race, the rule is that you must keep one foot on the ground at all times. In other words, you must not lift your back foot up until you've put your front foot down. Your back leg must also be straightened for a moment while your back foot is on the ground. Have a go — it's not as easy as it sounds, especially if you're trying to walk quickly.

WARNING SIGNALS

Judges keep a close eye on the walkers. If a competitor is spotted breaking the rules, the judge will show a disc as a warning. If the competitor then commits a second offence, another disc will be raised signalling that he has been disqualified.

Medal-winning walkers achieve an average speed of more than 15 km/h — that's half as fast as a sprint champion but twice as fast as an Olympic swimmer!

SUPER STATS

WOMEN'S RECORDS - WORLD: **20-km**: Olimpiada Ivanova (RUS) 1 hr. 25 mins. 41 sec. / **50-km**: No world record exists.
OLYMPIC: **20-km**: Liping Wang (CHN) 1 hr. 29 mins. 5 sec. / **50-km**: No world record exists.

THE MARATHON

The marathon is a gruelling 42-km run through the streets of the Olympic city. It's the ultimate test of stamina and determination!

BY ROYAL COMMAND

The first modern Olympic marathons were 40 km long. However, when the Games came to London in 1908, the race was lengthened slightly to 42.195 km. This was because the British royal family wanted to watch the start of the race in front of Windsor Castle! This distance was then adopted as the official length of the Olympic marathon.

ANIMAL OLYMPIANS

When it comes to marathon journeys, the Caribou annual trip across North America takes some beating. These large deer travel up to 40,000 km every year - the equivalent of almost 1,000 marathon races.

40,000 km

Naoko Takahashi (JPN)

NOT FAIR!

Dorando Pietri (ITA) was the unluckiest marathon runner in Olympic history. At the Games in 1908, Pietri was leading the race as he entered the Olympic stadium. However, he collapsed from exhaustion four times on the final lap of the track. Eventually, two race officials helped him across the finish line. Although Pietri finished first he was disqualified — because the judges said he had 'used external support' which is against the rules!

Dorando Pietri (ITA)

TIRED YET?

Naoko Takahashi (JPN), pictured left, celebrates as she crosses the finish line during the women's Marathon final at the Sydney Olympic Games. Takahashi still holds the women's Olympic record for the event.

THIRSTY WORK

Officials hand out drinks of water to the runners 11 km into the race and then at every 5 km or so after that. Wet sponges are also handed out at regular intervals to help keep the runners cool.

DID YOU KNOW?

🎽 The first ever modern Olympic marathon was won by a penniless Greek shepherd in 1896. As well as a gold medal, he was presented with a horse and cart for his village!

🎽 Marathon world and Olympic records are regarded as 'unofficial' because each marathon course is slightly different.

🎽 In the 1988 marathon, 118 runners took part — the largest number of people ever to compete in a single Olympic event!

INDEX

Acknowledgements

We would like to thank Ian Hodge, Richard Mead and Elizabeth Wiggans for their assistance.
Cartoons by John Alston.
Copyright © 2000 ticktock Entertainment Ltd.
Revised edition 2008 ticktock Media Ltd., 2 Orchard Business Centre, North Farm Road, Tunbridge Wells, TN2 3XF, UK.

A CIP catalogue record for this book is available from the British Library.
ISBN 978 1 84696 730 6

Picture Credits: All images courtesy of Allsport, except for Lutz Bongarts/ Bongarts/ Getty Images: 30. Matthew Fearn/ PA Archive/ PA Photos: 16/17. Gouhier- Kempinaire/ Cameleon/ ABACA/ PA Photos: 12/13c. Dave and Les Jacobs/ Getty Images: OFC. Glyn Kirk/ Action Plus: 18/19c. Sipa Press/ Rex Features: 27br.

Picture research by Image Select. Printed in China.